Praise for

"So much wisdom written inside…"

"Beautiful and Timely"

"Inspirational"

"This is a great book for anyone trying to find meaning or inspiration. Highly recommended."

"This book is… one that you will probably be revisiting and re-reading…"

Also by Blake Wm. Halladay

ascend

30 Days to Respecting and Loving Yourself!

Dear God,

Dear God,

A year-long journey of vulnerability, discovery, and faith.

By Blake Wm. Halladay

A YOUniversity Press book

Copyright © 2023 by Blake Wm. Halladay

All rights reserved.

No part of this content may be modified or altered in any form whatsoever, electronic, or mechanical, including photocopying, recording, or by any informational storage or retrieval system without express written, dated and signed permission from the author.

DISCLAIMER AND/OR LEGAL NOTICES: The information presented herein represents the view of the author as of the date of publication. Because of the rate with which conditions change, the author reserves the right to update his opinion based on new conditions. While every attempt has been made to verify the information provided in this work, neither the author nor his affiliates/partners assume any responsibility for errors, inaccuracies, or omissions. Any slights of people or organizations are unintentional. If counsel concerning mental health or related matters is needed, the services of a fully qualified professional should be sought. This work is not intended for use as a source of mental health therapy or counseling. Any reference to any person or business whether living or dead is purely coincidental.

TheYOUniversity Press

To Adam.

For showing us all what courage looks like.

Contents

Introduction 13
   Who? How? 15
   Not a Journal 19

Part One, The Journey Begins 23
   "Dear God, I always wanted to tell you…" 25
   "I'm mad at You because…" 29
   "Why did You…?" 35
   "Did You hear the one about…?" 39
   "When I was a little child…" 43
   "The last few years have been…" 49
   "I always wished I had done…" 53
   "Something I don't understand is…" 59
   "I'm struggling with…" 65
   "I'm looking forward to…" 69
   "These next few years are going to be…" 75
   "I felt alone when…" 81
   "I knew You were with me when…" 87
   "I'm worried about…" 93
   "I'm so grateful for…" 99
   "I can't seem to find peace because…" 105
   "I felt so peaceful when…" 111
   "What do You want me to do about…?" 117
   "Why did _____ have to happen?" 123
   "I love it when You…" 129
   "Please help me understand…" 135

"I don't know what to feel about…" 141
"Thank You for teaching me about…" 147
"Thank You for teaching me how to…" 153
"I'm pretty good at…" 159
"I'm not so good at…" 165

Part Two, Growth and Awakening 171

Second Chances 173
"Dear God, I always wanted to tell you…" 177
"I'm mad at You because…" 181
"Why did You…?" 187
"Did You hear the one about…?" 191
"When I was a little child…" 195
"The last few years have been…" 201
"I always wished I had done…" 205
"Something I don't understand is…" 211
"I'm struggling with…" 217
"I'm looking forward to…" 221
"These next few years are going to be…" 227
"I felt alone when…" 233
"I knew You were with me when…" 239
"I'm worried about…" 245
"I'm so grateful for…" 251
"I can't seem to find peace because…" 257
"I felt so peaceful when…" 263
"What do You want me to do about…?" 269
"Why did _____ have to happen?" 275
"I love it when You…" 281
"Please help me understand…" 287
"I don't know what to feel about…" 293
"Thank You for teaching me about…" 299

"Thank You for teaching me how to…" 305

Part Three, Love and Gratitude 311

The Last Part, or The First 313
"I Love You." 315
"Thank You for loving me." 319

Final Thoughts 325

Ponder 327

Introduction

Who? How?

One question: what does it mean to know God?

If you're like me, you grew up in a culture that constantly emphasized how important it is to know God, but at the same time never really explained exactly how to do that. I heard it all the time, it's the first great commandment, right? To love God with all my heart, soul, and mind? Great, sounds awesome. But how exactly do I *do* that? How do I love someone I believe is there, someone I believe to be all-powerful, someone I'm told loves me eternally, but yet at the same time is someone who sometimes seems incredibly distant and unknowable?

Don't get me wrong, I love where I grew up. There are a ton of benefits of being in such a faith-filled culture, but like you and everyone else, there were things I had to learn for myself. Honestly, for much of my younger life I didn't think much of what it meant to know God, or even to know myself really. I went through life like the rest of the world, just going through the motions trying to survive another day. But as life marched on, and the world got crazier, something inside of me changed. Something opened up in my soul. Something deep. Something that craved to really know who I was and to really know the one who supposedly loved me more than anyone else. I craved that knowledge. I craved that love. Perhaps it was because I started to see my own failings more, my own weaknesses and shortcomings; I wanted to know the purpose of it all and if I really could be loved in spite of all of that. I craved a relationship with someone who could love me unconditionally, regardless of how imperfect I was.

Somewhere during that time is when it hit me. I mean really hit me. I had been looking at this all wrong. I had been viewing the goal of knowing God as a solitary goal, meaning a goal that I had to achieve all by myself. I had never consciously thought of my relationship with God as just that: a *relationship*. A relationship with two people, not just one. I came to realize that I was just as important in that relationship as I believed my Father in Heaven to be. Suddenly, in the grand eternal plan, *I* mattered.

That awareness, that awakening of a hint of my own value, started me on a journey of true understanding and love. I began to understand that the purpose of the first great commandment was very different than I had grown up believing. I began to understand what the purpose of it all was, that the reason He wants me to love Him is so that I can understand just how much *He* loves *me*. *I* was the missing piece all along. I didn't know myself, and He was showing me the way. <u>I began to understand that the path to *me*, was through *Him*.</u>

I began to understand that if I wanted to love with all my heart, soul, and mind, I needed to understand what that kind of love looked like and felt like, and the only person I knew of who already had that kind of love, was Him. If I could let God show me how much He loves *me*, I would be able to finally understand how to not only love Him in return, but finally come to fully deeply love myself as well. I began to understand that those two seemingly separate ideas (loving Him vs. loving me) were actually inextricably combined into one great truth: *to love Him, is to love me, and to love me, is to love Him.*

That new awareness began to guide my journey, and as I tried to move into a life of greater connection, I realized that I had some work to do. I realized that there were parts of me that I had never allowed myself to share with God in either prayer or conversation. Honestly, I realized there were parts of me that I hadn't consciously allowed myself to acknowledge even existed.

As I began to accept those parts of me, an interesting thing happened. Thoughts started to flow into my mind, promptings really, that challenged so many of the messages I had received from the somewhat orthodox society I grew up in. Promptings that pushed me towards new levels of faith and vulnerability that I didn't know were achievable. Many of these promptings challenged beliefs that I had held onto for most of my life. I started asking questions like, "is it okay that I'm mad at God sometimes?" and "is it okay that I worry or have fear?", which were inevitably followed up with, "Do these questions mean I don't love Him?"

Anger, worry, and doubt had always been signs of a lack of faith, or so I believed. But once I started accepting those parts of me and started sharing them with God, I found something that changed me forever: I found the truth. The truth that God loves me even if I'm not perfect, even if I worry about random silly things, even if I don't understand some parts of His gospel, even if my thoughts don't always "toe the line," even if I'm weak or make mistakes sometimes. *Even if I'm mad at Him.*

That truth helped me, for the first time in my life to begin to understand what it means to love myself, because for the first time in my life, I started really truly openly sharing all of myself with the one being who loves me more than anyone else. And you know what happened when I started sharing more of myself with God? He accepted me. All of me. He showed me that He loves me. The imperfect, fallible, sometimes fearful, sometimes grumpy, sometimes worrisome me. Me.

No matter what I threw at Him, no matter what I told Him, no matter how confused, sad, or angry I got, I felt Him sit with me, and love me. I felt my faith and connection to Him grow. I felt myself change and my light increase. I began to see myself and the world around me differently. And for the first time in my life, I began to understand the real purpose for the first great commandment:

That by loving Him, I could finally see that He loves *me* with all *His* heart, with all *His* soul, and with all *His* mind.

Not a Journal

This book is not a journal, it's a journey. It is not meant to be a place where you record the comings and goings of your day. It is not meant to be a place to record your favorite quotes or memes. Those are great things, but save them for your actual journal. This book rather is a map; a map to guide you on your journey of vulnerability and faith.

Within these pages you will find promptings designed to help you have conversations with God you've never had before. Some of those conversations will be scary, some will be hard, others will be light and fun. Some conversations will be about topics you have been afraid to tell Him about, others will be about topics you may have just never thought of discussing with Him. Whatever they are, they will help you draw closer to Him while simultaneously helping you to know and love yourself at a deeper level.

This book contains 52 conversations, one for each week of the year. Don't be too hung up on the timing though. You could do this in 52 days if you want, though I don't recommend it (some of these topics will take you some time to ponder before you can have an open conversation with God). Go at whatever pace you feel prompted to go at, but a week per conversation has a good flow. You may take less time on some conversations, and more on others. That's okay. No pressure. Just remember to be open and real. Let your heart and mind do the work and don't hold anything back. As I said before, this journey is one of vulnerability, discovery, and faith. The more vulnerable you are, the more you will discover, and the more your faith will grow.

How you conduct these conversations is up to you (i.e. out loud, in your head, in a quiet room, while listening to music, etc.), but I suggest that you set aside dedicated time each day to have a conversation with your Father in Heaven. If you struggle remembering to do things (that's me!), set a reminder on your phone at a specific time of day to have your conversation with God.

I recommend that you read the week's prompting on Sunday, and then let your mind and spirit contemplate the topic throughout the week. I'm not really a morning person, so I find that I have better conversations with Him in the evening after my subconscious has had a chance to ponder the topic throughout the day. You may find that you are too tired in the evenings, and mornings may work better for you. Whatever system works for you is fine. If you have to change things up along the way because something isn't working, that's fine too. Remember, no shame here. There is no right or wrong way to do this.

The only thing that will get in your way on this journey is not allowing yourself to be open and vulnerable with God. But again, no shame. If you find yourself meeting subconscious resistance, try to push through and see what comes. If you still aren't feeling it, no worries. Put the book aside and come back to it later when you feel ready. The Spirit will prompt you when it's time.

I have included lined pages after each week's conversation prompting for you to use as you see fit. Some prefer to write out their thoughts and feelings before they converse with God so they have specific points to share. Some prefer to wing it and let the conversation flow as the thoughts come and then record their insights after. Whatever works for you is great. You may end up trying many different methods until you find something that feels comfortable. That's just fine.

I would recommend however, that you at least write something down each week. Writing out your thoughts will help train your brain into action mode, which will then help your subconscious open up those long-closed memories and beliefs. Even if you only write a few sentences, that's enough to get things started.

There are multiple sections of conversations in this book. You will repeat most of the conversations in the second half of the year that you had in the first. That's by design. The first half of this journey will help you build new skills that will enable you to be much more open and honest with yourself and with God. When you come to the second half, you will find your conversations will flow more naturally and at a deeper level. Those more mature conversations will carry greater power towards change and spiritual growth.

In Part Two, have your conversation first, then look back at the first time you had that conversation and see just how much you've grown in the months that have passed. Pay attention to how your conversations have changed. I think you will be pleasantly surprised, and that's a very validating and motivating experience. Most of the conversations will be very different the second time through as you find new depths of vulnerability and faith in your soul.

I'm excited for you. I'm praying for you. This is not an easy journey, but it is a necessary one if you want to finally find peace. But I think, deep down, you already know that.

Ready? Remember, God is with you.
You got this.
"Dear God…"

Part One,
The Journey Begins

"Dear God, I always wanted to tell you…"

For your very first week, I want you to rip the bandaid off and get right to it. I want you to sit down and tell God something you have never told Him before. The topic of conversation can be either light or heavy, it really depends on what you're feeling this week, but if I were to encourage you one way or the other (if you really aren't feeling compelled in either direction), I would encourage you to go deep.

What is it that you've always wanted to tell Him that you never have?

What is it that's been sitting in the back of your mind, or in the deepest parts of your heart, that you've always wanted to bring out and put into words to Him? To the one who loves you most? To the one who is always there and doesn't care what you did or did not do?

When you say these words, "Dear God, I always wanted to tell you…" what feelings stir in your heart?

Is there something heavy that you've wanted to share with Him but just haven't? Something that you've held onto for years but just never felt the courage to speak out loud or to write down?

Or is it something lighter or something funny?

Take some time this week to really think about this, to really think about the things you've always wanted to tell Him but maybe felt like you couldn't, for whatever reason.

Often times societal constructs get in the way of our conversations with God. You may have been told that you *can't* say certain things to Him, or that you *shouldn't* say certain things to Him. This is your week to throw all that out the window. Challenge those messages this week and tell Him exactly what you've always wanted Him to know.

I always wanted to tell You...

"I'm mad at You because..."

This can be a really hard week for many people, because the very idea of being mad at God seems unrighteous or inappropriate. I understand that personally as I carried the same mentality for many years of my life. It wasn't until I really started to understand His perfect love for me that I started to understand that He was going to love me no matter what, even though there were things that I was very frustrated with Him over. There were angers that I was carrying in my heart, because of things in my life that had happened, or things that I didn't understand, and when I finally allowed myself to acknowledge that I was upset at God for a lot of those things, I found a whole new level of freedom with Him. The doors were swung wide open (or at least they were more open than they were before). This change gave me more freedom in truly talking to Him, and in return, I gained more freedom in truly *hearing* Him.

What I found through my anger was peace and understanding, because when I finally started to talk to Him about the things that I was mad at Him for, I really started to understand how His perfect love was taking affect in my life, and how those very things were placed in my life to help me grow and become a better, kinder, more loving person. It may sound counterintuitive to you, especially if you grew up in a society that shuns this level of open emotional sharing, but you *will* find peace through your anger. When you finally break free and allow yourself to share *all* emotions with Him, including your perceived "negative" emotions, you will find more peace than you ever knew was possible.

This week, I challenge you to truly be vulnerable in your conversations with God. Let Him have it, really. Tell Him how angry you are, and why. I promise you, He is there to hear you, I promise you that you will not get lost in your anger, rather you will find pieces of you that you had long forgotten.

He loves you, even when you're mad at Him.

I'm mad at You because...

"Why did You…?"

The big question: "Why did You?" This question has plagued humanity since the dawning of time. There are so many things we do not understand, so many pieces of God's greater puzzle that are just eluding our grasp. This week is the time to find closure, if possible. Take the time to really think about the events in your life that you don't understand, events that you still struggle to see God's hands in, and take those events to Him in prayer and in conversation. Ask Him why He did whatever it is He did. Ask Him why He allowed whatever it is He allowed. Or why He didn't do or didn't allow whatever it is He didn't do or didn't allow. His door is always open for you, ask Him whatever questions you need.

Heads up, as you sit and ponder this question this week, you will find that there are probably more times in your life that you want to ask Him about than you realize. So go for it. Open up the conversation with Him this week and ask Him why He did whatever it is you are wondering or concerned about. Get personal. Get it off your chest. Remove the burden from your shoulders. Let it all out.

You will find closure here, if you are open to what that closure may look like, because it may not come in the form that you had expected, or even hoped for. Sometimes closure comes from His reminder that His ways are higher than our ways and we just don't know everything He knows. Sometimes closure is found in simply trusting that He knows what He's doing.

He's got this, and He's got you.

Why did You...?

"Did You hear the one about…?"

Joke time! This week is a lighthearted and fun week. Sometimes we forget that we can talk to God in the good times as well as in the bad times, in the light times as well as in the dark times. This week is here to just remind you that He's always there and He always wants to hear from you, even when things are going great. We want to get to the point where we can share every emotion with Him, even laughter and excitement. You've worked pretty hard on tearing down barriers and learning to share deeper harder emotions with Him, so this week just have some fun and take some time to share your favorite jokes with Him (they don't all have to start with "Did you hear the one about…?"!). By the end of the week you should find yourself a little more comfortable to share a little more emotion with Him, even the silly emotions.

Did You hear the one about...?

"When I was a little child…"

We all have something in our past that brings us heartbreak and turmoil in our present. We all have something from our childhood that is confusing, hurtful, or even traumatic. This week is an opportunity for you to go back to your roots with God, to share with Him those things that you remember from the earliest years of your life that played a foundational role in who you are today and how your life is turning out. Some of those things are going to be good and happy memories, some of them will be the exact opposite.

I highly recommend you take some time before you sit down with Him to ponder on this statement: "When I was a little child…" If you've been writing your conversations down in the mornings, perhaps change to the evenings for this week and allow your mind a full day to ponder what things you want to talk to Him about from your childhood. Often we need that extra time for our minds to open themselves up to those old memories, because often we have *subconsciously* shut them down so that we don't *consciously* have to deal with them in our present adult lives, but just because we aren't consciously aware of them doesn't mean they aren't still affecting us.

Start each morning reminding yourself to think about things that happened when you were a little child; give yourself permission to go back there. Give yourself permission to open those memories back up again so that you can process them together with your Father in Heaven. Then let the process do its work. Trust that the memories will be there when you need them.

When the time comes that you have set apart to have this conversation, find a place where you can sit quietly, and then begin telling Him about whatever it is that comes to your mind. If you normally don't like to have your conversations with God out loud, that's fine, but maybe for this one at least vocalize the words, "When I was a little child," and then let your inner mind do the rest. You'll be surprised what happens when you just say those few words out loud. You'll be surprised at the memories that come.

Share them all with Him, He wants to hear them, because remember, He was there too.

When I was a little child...

"The last few years have been…"

The last few years have been… what? Have they been good? Have they been bad? Have they been awful? Have they been great?

How have things gone the last few years? You've spent some time talking about what life was like when you were little, so how's it going now? Did things happen in the last few years the way you expected them to? Or did they take an unexpected turn that you hadn't planned on? How exactly has life been going?

Most adults, when prompted with this sentence, will usually find that the last few years have been a little tough, but why is that? Why is life so often difficult as an adult? How would it have been different if you had a better, more open relationship with God throughout the last few years? Have those years really been as tough as you thought they were? Or could they have been better? All questions to ponder this week as you think about what you want to talk to God about the last few years.

Maybe the last few years have been really great, and you just want to tell Him thank you for that. Or maybe the last few years have really been tough and hard and you want to share your emotions about that with Him. Either way, just get real. Don't try to sugarcoat it, and don't try to over-inflate it. Be honest about what the last few years were really like, and talk to Him about it.

Then listen to hear His perspective.

These last few years have been...

"I always wished I had done…"

We hear a lot in the self development world that we shouldn't have regrets. Well, that's all fine and dandy, but it isn't realistic. Whether we should or shouldn't have them is irrelevant this week, because the truth of the matter is we usually do have them whether we admit it or not.

I fully agree with living life in the present and seeing our past experiences as steppingstones along our path to growth and peace; I believe that wholeheartedly and teach it often. However, that doesn't mean that the regrets we have just magically disappear. It's natural to have feelings of sadness and grief. Those are natural human emotions when we feel like we have missed out on something we wanted to take part in. The only way to resolve those emotions is to let ourselves feel them, to welcome them in, to love them while they're here, and then when the time comes, send them lovingly on their way.

No shaming yourself this week, okay? Share the things with God that you always wished you had done in your life. Share the events you wish you had attended, the topics you wish you had studied, the talents you wish you had developed, whatever it is that you wish you had always done, but never got a chance to. Open your heart to Him and share the memories, the thoughts, the feelings, and the regrets.

This doesn't have to be a deep and heavy week. Depending on where you are at, it may or may not be. If you aren't feeling deep heaviness about the things you wish you had always done, that's great. Go with that. Share with Him in a lighthearted manner.

Who knows? Maybe by sharing these things with Him this week, you will find the motivation and the opportunity to do some of them that are still available and turn them from regrets into accomplishments!

I always wished I had done...

"Something I don't understand is…"

I know I use this term a lot, but this week is a week of *vulnerability*. Many of us were brought up in cultures (religious cultures especially), that do not support the idea of questioning what you have been taught. Whether the religion itself preaches that mentality or not, it's often present in the culture that surrounds the religious teachings. If this applies to you, then this will be another week of challenging societal norms, of challenging the system.

Dedicate your conversations this week solely to the things you don't understand about His plan, and to the questions you have about the doctrine you've been taught. Only you can tell how strong the societal pull is within your heart and your mind, so only you will know how hard you're going to have to fight to ask those questions this week.

Perhaps it's easy for you to acknowledge the things that you don't understand in God's great plan; if so, I applaud you for that. This week will flow a little more easily for you. However, if you are like the many people who struggle with admitting that you don't understand all of the aspects of God's gospel, then this week may be a little bit harder for you in terms of opening up and really sharing your confusion with Him.

As in other weeks, I remind you that He loves you and that He wants to hear from you. There is no question you can ask Him that will offend Him. God does not have an ego. Anytime we come to Him is a time He cherishes. He knows we aren't perfect and He is ever patient with us.

You may find that you need a couple of days before you can actually sit down and have this conversation with Him, that's okay. When you get there, do the best you can to open the floodgates and let your feelings flow. Tell Him what it is you don't understand about His gospel and explain that you need some help coming to terms with some things. Again, be vulnerable and honest.

Also, remember that faith has a large component of "not knowing." It's okay if you don't understand everything, some things are just too big to understand. That doesn't mean that He doesn't want you to come to Him and ask Him about them. Give Him a chance this week. Give Him the chance to help you resolve some of your questions about His teachings (or the teachings you have been taught about Him by others).

Something I don't understand is...

"I'm struggling with…"

What is bothering you?

What is troubling your heart?

What are the things that are sitting in your subconscious that just can't seem to find resolution?

What are the roadblocks in your life right now?

Is there something you're struggling with mentally?

Emotionally?

Spiritually?

Are you struggling with something about yourself and your own identity?

Are you struggling to develop a certain skill or aptitude that you feel will make you successful?

Are you struggling with a portion of your faith?

Are there questions that you have about God and His gospel that you just can't seem to reconcile?

Do you worry that you are weak, or that you in someway don't match up to the perceived standards of the world?

(Or the perceived standards of what it *looks like* to live a God-centered life?)

Be open and honest with God this week about whatever it is you are struggling with. Remember not to shame yourself or your worries, no concern is too small for Him. He loves all parts of you. Give Him a chance to hear you, and then give Him a chance to send you peace.

I'm struggling with...

"I'm looking forward to…"

This week is a bit of a change of pace from the previous weeks. You've had a lot of really deep discussions with God lately and I'm sure many of those have been pretty heavy. That's good, those are often the conversations that we really need to have in order to tear down the walls inside of us that keep us from truly being vulnerable with Him and coming to understand our own worth. That being said, we want to change things up a little bit this week.

Our relationship with God is not meant to only be heavy; in fact, it's meant to be joyful. The heavy discussions are some of the keys that open the doors to a more joyful God-centered existence by allowing us to finally be fully vulnerable, but those are not the only conversations we need to be having. This week is about hope.

Like other weeks, this may be easy for you, or it may be hard for you, depending on where you are right now on your spiritual journey. If you are in a hopeful, forward-looking place, great, share everything with Him that you are excited for regarding the future. If however, you are struggling with the present, then the future is likely to look bleak and feel even bleaker, and this may be a harder topic for you to tackle. That's okay. Remember never to shame yourself for the way you are currently feeling. Just get curious about it instead.

If you're struggling with the future, take some time before writing your conversations with God this week to meditate, ponder, and even daydream about a hopeful future. The future isn't set in stone, and often all it takes for the hope and happiness wheels to be set in motion is for us to bring our desired goodness into the light. Meditating, pondering, and dreaming are all tools we have at our disposal to bring our deep hopes from the darkness of our hidden minds into the light of possibility and potential.

Start each day with this sentence in mind: "God, I'm really looking forward to...," and you may be surprised at what will emerge from places in your heart that you didn't know were there.

I'm looking forward to...

"These next few years are going to be…"

Another forward looking week. However, this week is without any sort of emotional prompting. I'm not going to prompt you with "looking forward…" or "struggling with…," or anything that will lead you one way or another. This week is a blank canvas where your spirit can paint whatever picture it feels. This is an opportunity for you to get in tune with yourself without much prompting from me.

When you say the words out loud "These next few years are going to be…" what emotions arise within you? Where in your body are you feeling those emotions? Pay attention to you body. Our bodies manifest emotions physically; that's literally why we call them "feelings." Practicing physical awareness can help you sift through the noise of the world and really tune in to what it is you are actually feeling. With that in mind, what sensations arise in the physical part of your being when you ponder this week's conversation?

Helpful questions to ponder:
Do you feel excited about the next couple of years?
Do you feel worried about the next few years?
Where do you notice these feelings in your body?
What do they feel like?
Do you feel a tingling or warming sensation somewhere?
Do you feel tension anywhere?
Do you feel a rushing sensation or an increased heart rate?
Do you feel nauseated?
Are you smiling?
Are you tired and worn out?

Or are you restless and filled with energy?

Most of the time we mortals are very out of touch with how our emotions manifest themselves physically. We often have too much going on around us, too much stimulation, to allow us to really focus inwardly and on our own experiences. Opening your spiritual eyes to the sensations that arise in your body with certain emotions can really help you tune in on exactly what it is you are feeling.

I know what it's like to be confused about my feelings. When I learned to be more aware of the physical sensations that partnered with the emotions I was feeling, it really helped me to sift through the messiness of life around me and become more aware of what it is I was actually feeling in those moments. This week let your body talk to your spirit about the feelings you carry deep down inside of you about the future. Then tell God what you came up with.

Again, blank canvas here. What do the next few years look like and feel like to you? Tell God all about it.

He already knows what the next few years are going to bring of course, but He wants to know what you think about it, and how you feel about it.

These next few years are going to be...

"I felt alone when…"

Loneliness is one of the heaviest feelings we can experience in this mortal life. Loneliness is often a strange phenomenon for us humans because we always seem to be physically surrounded by other people, and yet even in the midst of the crowds and the hustle and bustle of life, we often feel very very alone. Loneliness is a universal feeling, which is somewhat ironic if you think about it. Everyone knows what it feels like to feel alone, and you would think that would help us all to have something to come together over, but yet loneliness still prevails.

When have you felt lonely?

Do you feel lonely now?

Why?

What's going on inside of you?

When you felt alone, what other feelings were you carrying at the same time?

What was the situation?

Were you surrounded by people and yet still felt as if you were metaphorically "alone on a deserted island?"

What was that like for you?

Were you able to come out of it?

If so, how?

Is there anything you learned during that time about yourself?

Any personal awarenesses?

Tell God about it. Tell Him everything. He knows what it feels like to feel alone. After all, He is the one that gave us the capacity to feel all of these emotions. There is no one better to hear you and comfort you in your loneliness than Him.

Bonus question: Have you ever pondered why God would allow us to feel lonely? Why we all have to feel alone at some point in our lives? It's an interesting question; one that most people have never truly pondered, at least not with the intent to learn. If you haven't ever done so, this week would be a good week to ask God what He thinks about it.

I felt alone when...

"I knew You were with me when…"

This week is the opposite side of the coin from loneliness, and serves as a natural outgrowth of your conversation last week. Who knows? In your conversation last week, you may have even found ways that He was with you in the midst of your loneliest times. If so, I applaud you, that's a beautiful thing. If not, that's okay. You had the conversation with Him last week that you needed to have, and that's exactly what it needed to be. You will have many more opportunities to talk with Him and to learn to see Him in your life, even in the darkest times. This week, focus on the opposite of loneliness, focus on presence.

When have you felt Him in your life?

When have you felt His presence?

When did you know that He was with you?

If you want to take that even further, how did you know that He was with you?

He has promised to always be with us, but it's not always easy to feel the manifestation of that promise (hence the "lonely" conversation last week), but this week is a chance for you to share with Him the times when you knew He was walking side-by-side with you down the path. Those are important memories and He would love to share in reminiscing about those times with you. Similar to a few weeks ago, this is a blank canvas.

What were the times like when you knew He was with you?

Were they good times?

Bad times?

Both?

Often we notice His presence best in the trying times because those are the times we are looking for Him most. If those are the times that you remember Him being with you, talk to Him about those times. Tell Him what you remember and how you knew He was with you.

For a challenge, try thinking about both difficult *and* easy times. Even though we tend to notice Him most in the difficult times, He is also with us in the easy times. We just tend to forget Him when life is going great. Try to find some times in your memory when you knew He was with you even when life was full of happiness and peace.

It's good for us to recognize His presence at all times, and not just when we feel like we need Him most.

I knew You were with me when...

"I'm worried about…"

Worry is a complex emotion, especially in religious cultures, because we are often subliminally taught that worry is bad because in some way worry shows a lack of faith. In some cultures the shame isn't even subliminal, it's right out in the open. That situation can be very conflicting for us, because just because people say "don't worry," doesn't mean worry magically goes away. Worrying is part of our default human experience. The problem is most people try to "encourage" those around them to not worry by trying to shame the worry out of them. This simply doesn't work.

We all worry. I do, every day. I'm getting better at it, but it's still there. The ironic thing with these types of topics is that the most effective way to stop worrying, begins with actually accepting and admitting that we are indeed worrying. When we accept ourselves just the way we are, it opens doors for us to elevate to entirely new levels.

This week I want you to start with openly accepting and allowing yourself to worry. Then take the most important step: Take those worries to God. Let Him know what it is you are carrying, what it is you are worried about. Just ramble it all out to Him, I promise He will never shame you for it. He already knows you're worried, so there's no sense in hiding it.

What are you worried about?

Is it something to do with your family?

Your friends?

Yourself?

Is it something to do with the world around you?

Politics?

Pop-culture?

School, work, or home duties?

Tell Him everything, let Him be in that worry with you, let Him walk that path with you, let Him guide you and comfort you. True peace comes from Him, but we will never know and be grateful for that peace unless we accept and share our worries and fears. Challenge the voices in your head, challenge the societal pressure, and just let yourself be.

Whatever it is, this week is a chance for you to just let it all flow with the one who loves you most.

I'm worried about...

"I'm so grateful for..."

Another opportunity for a "heart dump" this week. Last week you had the opportunity to tell God what was weighing on your heart, this week is the flip side of that discussion. What are the things in your life that you are grateful for that maybe you never expressed to Him?

Take a deep breath and close your eyes for just a moment. Try to clear your mind from all the hustle and bustle of the day. Now open your eyes and take a look around you. See how blessed you are. If you allow yourself, you will see an abundance of blessings right before your eyes. Blessings you experience every single day.

Do you have clothes?

Do you have electricity?

Do you have water?

What do you see in just the room you are currently sitting in?

How are those things blessings to you?

Now take the next moment to express gratitude to God for the all the blessings you see and feel. It doesn't matter how simple you may feel the blessing is, share your gratitude for it with Him. Even if all you can say is, "Thank you," that's enough.

Note: It's Okay to ask Him for inspiration on how to share your blessings with those who aren't as fortunate as you are, but that's not the purpose of this week. It's often difficult for us to just be grateful for what we have without shaming ourselves because we have more than someone else. That happens a lot in religious cultures. It's a good thing to want to bless others and to want others to have blessed easy peaceful lives, but this week is about you putting aside shame and expressing gratitude for what you have.

There will come a time and a place to ask for inspiration on how to help others, but this week I want you to just focus on *your* life and the blessings that surround *you* each and every day. Think about your body, your mind, your spirit, your lifestyle, your friends, your family, your job, your education, your hobbies and activities, and anything else you can think of where you can see blessings.

It's okay if you don't feel gratitude in all of those areas right now, they're just suggestions to help you start to think about the different ways that God has blessed you in this life. This week, take time to just say, "Thank you." Tell Him what you're grateful for. It doesn't matter if it's some huge life-changing thing or if it's as simple as seeing your favorite ice cream flavor at the grocery store. (What an amazing blessing that is!)

Open your heart and let the gratitude flow. You'll be amazed at how good you feel at the end of this week.

I'm so grateful for...

"I can't seem to find peace because…"

We live in very turbulent times. It seems that every day news reports and social media posts highlight another disagreement, another argument, and/or another fight between various groups of people who subscribe to different ways of thinking. These reports and posts send a message that our world is constantly divided and ever in turmoil. So many of us struggle to find peace in our lives because of this never ending onslaught of negativity and division in the world around us.

However, maybe the lack of peace you are currently feeling stems from something a bit closer to home for you than the national and world news. Perhaps there is discord in your own family. Or perhaps there is discord within your own soul.

What is it that is making you restless?

What is it that has stolen your hope for peace?

Is it the noise in the world around you?

Or is it something more intimate and private?

God has promised us peace when we turn to Him, but for most of us that can be a pretty elusive promise. His peace is different than our peace. His peace is grounded in an eternal perspective, a perspective that knows all things and how all things will progress. You and I do not have that same eternal perspective, simply because we are mortal.

Talk to Him this week about the restlessness you are feeling. Really dig into the reasons that you just can't seem to find peace in your life.

What is it that keeps you up at night?

What is it that worries you in the back of your mind all day long?

Be open and vulnerable with Him this week about your difficulties finding calm and rest so you can begin to find the path to the peace you seek.

I can't seem to find peace because...

"I felt so peaceful when…"

In contrast to the restlessness you talked to God about last week, this week take some time to ponder on the times in your life when you *did* feel peace.

What was happening?

What was the world like around you?

Was it any different?

Or were *you* different?

If so, why?

What was different about you in the times when you felt at peace?

Was there something happening inside of you then that isn't now?

Did you have a different relationship with God then than you do now?

We know that the world cannot bring us peace, it will forever be in turmoil due to its ever-changing and imperfect nature. Peace comes from within. Peace comes from our ability to communicate with God, and to hear His voice. Peace comes from being in His presence where we know that everything will work out exactly as it is meant to be. In His presence we are reminded that because He loves us eternally, everything in our lives is meant to one day bring us true and everlasting joy.

As you ponder this week about the times when you felt peaceful, ponder about *why* you felt peaceful in those times vs. the times where you felt restless. Focus on what was going on inside you rather than what was happening around you. As you talk to God about the times when you felt peaceful, ask Him to help you understand why you felt that way, and how you can maintain that feeling in your life.

Remembering and understanding the peaceful times will help you better find peace in the restless tumultuous times.

I felt so peaceful when...

"What do You want me to do about…?"

Him? Her? It? That situation that happened last week? That situation that's coming up soon? That work situation? That home situation?

What are you unsure about and need help/guidance with? It doesn't have to be anything big; remember, God wants to hear from us in all things. He cares about every detail of our lives, no matter how big or how small.

If there is something in your life that you don't know how to handle at the moment, talk to Him about it. Ask Him what He wants you to do about it. Then listen for His answer.

There are three steps in this conversation that are all equally important: talking, listening, and doing. If you struggle with the talking part, with asking for help and advice, then this is an opportunity for you to practice opening up and expressing your confusion or worry about life in a safe place. There is no safer place than God. This week, practice asking Him for advice. You will learn to hear and see His answers in time.

If on the other hand, you are pretty good at asking others for help, then focus this week on the *listening* and *doing* steps. Ask Him what He wants you to do, then be quiet and listen for His answers. If nothing comes right away, keep your eyes open and look for His answers in your life around you. Often He sends answers through other people, so make sure you are paying attention when interacting with others.

Once you receive an answer, get up and do it! If you ask Him what He wants you to do about something, and He tells you, then it's on you to make it happen. Hop to it, and do it. (Reminder: if you are scared to do what He asks, it's totally okay to ask Him for courage. He won't leave you alone.)

Again, this doesn't have to be something huge this. In fact, if you aren't used to asking for help, it's probably best to start with something small until you feel more comfortable. Either way, no matter how big or how small the issue, He wants to help so be sure to look and listen for His answers. Once you start to recognize His answers, you will start to see them more and more in your everyday life.

Eventually, you will see Him everywhere.

What do You want me to do about...?

"Why did _____ have to happen?"

We all have events in our lives, that we just don't know what to do with. Sometimes things happen that seem so far outside our understanding of God's plan that they can prove very shaking to our faith. Sometimes, because those events can be so confusing and painful, they end up being the very reason that we don't talk to Him anymore.

Some things are just too difficult for us to understand in the moment and that's what this week is all about. It's about the big confusions. It's about those events that happened in your life or in the lives of those around you that you just can't come to terms with, that you just can't seem to reconcile with your understanding of God and His nature.

First of all, give yourself permission to be confused. It's okay. Sometimes, living and growing up in very religious cultures can have a stifling effect on our vulnerability with God because we adopt the false belief that we are never allowed to have questions. I am telling you right now, *it's okay to not know the reasons for everything*, it doesn't mean that you are any less faithful. It doesn't mean that you are sinning or bad in someway. It simply means that you are human, and because you are human, it's sometimes difficult to see with an eternal perspective and understand how everything fits into a grand eternal plan.

Be patient and compassionate with yourself, especially in the areas where you feel most tender, which often include the types of situations where you just don't know why something had to happen. Be ready for some tears this week. This may be a hard week for you as you acknowledge those feelings and hard memories that are still lurking in the back of your mind. It's time to shed light on them and ask God to give you some peace and some understanding about why those events had to happened.

Just remember, I know this is hard, but remember that you may not get the answers you seek. Remember that His ways are not our ways, and sometimes the things that He needs to do are just too big for us to fully understand. That is why we are asked to have faith. Sometimes we just need to believe that everything happens for a reason, and leave it at that. If that's the case for you this week, if you don't get an answer to your question about why something had to happen the way it happened, then ask Him for peace instead.

Cry those tears out with Him. Ask Him all the questions. And then in the end, ask Him for help to believe that all things happen for our good, even the things you don't understand.

Then ask Him for help to let it go.

You got this.

Why did ____ have to happen?

"I love it when You…"

Finally, a happy week, right? After last week, you may need it to regain some sanity! Share some happiness with God this week. Let Him know what you think and feel about the good times in your life.

What are you grateful to Him for doing for you?

What does He do in your life that puts a smile on your face every time it happens?

Share those moments with Him this week. Fair warning, you may struggle with this for a bit, and that's okay. It's human nature to not consciously dwell on the good things in our lives. We are more wired to see and remember the location of a poisonous spider in our garden than to remember the locations of all the beautiful flowers. Don't shame yourself if you need a few minutes to come up with the good times.

Remembering and sharing positivity is a muscle that all of humanity needs to exercise; it just doesn't come easy to most of us. The good thing is once the good memories start flowing, they will begin to flow more and more easily, which will have a lasting positive effect on your life. If you need to, start with something small: "I love it when You wake me up two minutes before the alarm clock so I don't get startled awake." "I love it when You send spring rainstorms to water the flowers." "I love it when You nudge me to say hi to someone on the street so they can know they aren't alone."

Ponder this week on the things you love that God does for you, and then be ready to have the happiness floodgates thrown open! Happiness begets happiness. Gratitude begets gratitude. The more things you come up with to tell Him you love, the more your brain will start to rewire towards a more positive mindset. And, since you are involving Him in this process, you are essentially invoking His power which will make those brain changes even more effective and long-lasting. I love that benefit of consecrating everything we do (and think), to Him. When we turn to Him, He gives us His power to make everything just work better. Pretty cool, huh?

So, what do you love that He does for you? Tell Him everything you come up with.

This will be a beautiful week for you.

I love it when You...

"Please help me understand..."

A few weeks ago you spent some time talking to God about why certain things had to happen in your life, or in the lives of others. You discussed things and events that you struggled to understand the meaning behind. A few weeks before that you asked him about doctrinal teachings you struggle to understand. In both of those conversations you practiced being open with Him about your questions and your insecurities, and you practiced understanding that having questions does not mean you lack faith, in fact asking questions is often how we build faith: exercised faith, not blind ignorant faith.

God does not want us to be ignorant. He does not want us to blindly follow Him, never learning His ways or getting to know His nature. Of course He wants us to trust Him if something comes up that is too big for us to understand, but He wants that trust to be exercised, to be used, not to be left ignorant and passive.

God wants us to build strong faith that will resist the test of time because we put the effort into building it. Blind faith is weak faith, and eventually will fail. He wants us to ask the questions so He can answer the ones we can understand, and so He can reassure us on the ones we can't.

This is another week of questioning. The previous topics were specifically about past events and doctrinal teachings that you don't understand, this week is much broader. This week is about *anything* you don't understand.

Is there something to do with the world around you that He created that you don't understand?

Something about the future and His plan of salvation and exaltation?

Is there something going on with a loved one in your life that you don't understand?

Something with work?

Or home?

Is it all of these things?

Whatever it is, take it to Him this week. Continue with the energy of open vulnerability that you have been building for weeks now.

Remember, it's not a sin to not understand.

Please help me understand...

"I don't know what to feel about…"

Numb…

We all know what it feels like to not feel anything. We know what it feels like to feel numb, to not know how we feel about a certain event, topic, discussion, principle, etc. We all know what it feels like to feel confused about our feelings. (That's a lot of feeling in our "not feeling" huh?)

It's okay. It's part of the process. Awakening is hard. Self-awareness is hard. Challenging societal norms is hard.

Before you started to open your spiritual eyes there were probably many things you felt simply because someone else told you to feel them. Our society loves to tell us what to think and how to feel, and frankly, many of us love to be told; it's easier that way. But it isn't happier.

Our spirits will never find peace in such a primal, basic state. We are meant to elevate. We are meant to grow, to learn, to feel. This week may involve some paradigm challenging for you. Get in tune with your spirit, with your soul, and seek out those places where you aren't really at peace with what you are being told to feel, the places where the "popular crowd" is telling you to feel a certain way but you just can't get on board.

Take those feelings and situations to God and ask *His* opinion on them. Ask for help to understand your real feelings, the feelings underneath all the noise from the world. Accept whatever comes. Remember, feelings are neither good nor bad, they just are. Don't judge your feelings, don't try to change them, just look for them and accept them. Take the situation to God, and ask for help to understand how you really feel.

Important Note: If the feelings that arose in you when you first read this week's prompt came from more of a traumatized place rather than a confused place, pay attention to that. Numbness can come for many reasons, and if you aren't feeling confused about societal paradigms, childhood messages, or the like, rather you are feeling numb because of a certain traumatic event that your mind and soul just can't come to terms with, take that awareness as a message that God wants you to heal from that trauma. It's okay to explore that with Him. However, you may want to also explore that with a trained professional. Therapy is a gift from God in many ways, I know mine has been.

Be kind to yourself. If you feel you need it, find someone trained to listen to your hurt, someone who will help walk you down the path of healing and peace. You deserve it.

I don't know what to feel about...

"Thank You for teaching me about…"

What is something that you are glad you know about now, that you didn't know about 10 years ago? 15 years ago?

Or even something you didn't know about yesterday, last week, or last month?

What is some bit of knowledge that has changed your life?

That has changed the way you see yourself, your fellow spiritual brothers and sisters, or the world the itself?

How has gaining this knowledge changed you?

What has happened differently in your life now that your eyes are opened?

Ponder this week on the things God has taught you about that have really had an impact on your life and your spirituality. Focus on knowledge, wisdom, awarenesses, etc. Don't focus on abilities or on things you are grateful for learning how to *do*, that's for next week. This week is for understandings, for wisdom gained, for knowledge that has changed your life.

If something immediately comes to mind, great, tell Him all about it and how grateful you are for it. If you're drawing a blank at the moment, that's okay. It often takes time to rewire our brains to focus more on the positives in our lives, so be kind to yourself if nothing comes quickly.

Grab out a piece of paper and a pen and start writing down awarenesses you have had throughout your life about yourself and about life in general. You will be surprised how things will start to flow once you put that pen to paper. So start writing and let them flow.

You'll know when something comes up that you want to talk to Him about, just pay attention to your feelings as you are writing. Once you have something, tell Him all about it. Tell Him why you are grateful for His teaching and how your life is better because of what you now know.

As with all the other weeks, this week is a week of self-awareness, but it's also a week of gratitude. Focus on just telling Him thank you this week. Try to stave off any questioning, complaining, or pleading. There is a time and a place for those things, but this week is for gratitude.

Sharing gratitude with God is a very enlightening experience, so open your heart with gratitude, and let the light in.

Thank You for teaching me about...

"Thank You for teaching me how to…"

As I mentioned last week, this week is about things God has taught you how to do, rather than things He has taught you to know or understand. This week is about sharing your gratitude for things you have learned how to do that have had a substantial impact on your life. As with other weeks, be careful not to get lost in "the big things," or the skills the world finds value in. Those things are great, and if you have some of them, fantastic; definitely include them in your gratitude conversations with God this week. But more often than not, those aren't the skills that benefit your life the most.

Most often the skills God has taught us that allow us to function in the quiet times are the ones that benefit our lives the most:

The skill to truly listen to someone and hear that person's story.

The skill of tuning into your own feelings and knowing your own heart.

The ability to know your personal worth in a sea of confusing values set by the world.

The skill to laugh instead of cry.

The skill to cry instead of laugh.

The skill of sitting quietly and feeling wonder in the world around you.

The skill to see good in others, especially when they are struggling to see it in themselves.

The skill of seeing light and purpose, when all around you seems dark.

All these amazing skills that God has taught you, often through very difficult times of your own. Whatever it is, share some gratitude with God for teaching you how to do it. Big or small. Light or heavy. Outward or inward. It doesn't matter what it is, if you are grateful you learned how to do it, then share that gratitude with Him.

This is going to be a wonderful conversation for you this week, I can feel it.

Thank You for teaching me how to...

"I'm pretty good at…"

It's bragging time. Seriously. It's time to list out everything you feel you are good at, and then tell God all about them. Don't sugar coat anything. Don't discount anything. Don't try to downplay your own greatness in favor or "humility," or to try to help someone else feel better. Discounting yourself is not true humility. True humility is connecting with God and accepting the truth for what it is, no more, no less. Don't add to the truth, and certainly don't take away from it.

Often growing up in very religious cultures, we inadvertently gain a certain understanding that somehow self-deprecation = humility. I'm telling you now, it doesn't. We are taught, either overtly or covertly, that acknowledging our own skills, traits, aptitudes, and God-given abilities somehow makes us prideful or vain. And we are all taught just how evil the sin of pride can be. Unfortunately, much of this is taught in error. Yes, it isn't good to be prideful, but pride doesn't just mean boasting or self-aggrandizing. Those can be parts of pride, yes, but pride in essence is merely our opposition to and rebellion against God's will.

Pride most often manifests itself in our refusal to acknowledge the aptitudes God gave us. If He gave you the talent to make others laugh, do you think it's His will that you hide that talent and never use it because you don't want to seem "prideful?" Most definitely not. Think of it this way: if pride is opposition to God, and humility is the opposite of pride, then what exactly is humility? Simple, it's connection. Specifically, it's connection to God and His will. The more connected you are to Him, the closer your relationship with Him becomes. The closer your relationship becomes, the more humble you become and the more you start to accept truth as it stands, neither adding to it nor taking away from it. That truth includes the truth about you and the greatness He put into you. The better you get to know Him, the better you get to know yourself. That is an eternal truth.

Don't worry about boasting or being prideful as you talk to Him this week, I'm pretty sure that's not a problem you struggle with anyway. In fact, I would daresay that it's much more likely that you often diminish yourself or try to downplay your talents and aptitudes, especially around others, am I right? I totally understand.

This week I want you to push through all those walls that are keeping you from accepting who you really are. Tear down all those barriers that are holding you back from believing in your own God-given greatness. It can take a lot of practice to get to a place of truthful humility, so it's okay if you have to puff up a little this week, it's okay to brag to Him. God knows your heart, He knows who you really are.

You are His child. You are safe with Him.

I'm pretty good at...

"I'm not so good at..."

Truth. Focus on truth. If you have to, reread the prompt from last week so you can remind yourself of what humility really looks like. Humility requires truth. I understand if you feel a very strong pull to create a giant list of things you think you aren't good at this week, especially coming off a week of focusing on your goodness and strength (it's natural to feel pulled to slip back into old habits of shrinking and self-denial), but I'm going to challenge you before you even get started here: are you being true? Are you really not good at all those things your mind wants to convince you of? Or have you been conditioned to believe that you are not good at them? Or at least to not admit that you are good at them?

You need to start this week with a certain level of suspicion. Suspicion of your own beliefs about your own skills, aptitudes, talents, etc., (or your perceived lack of those things). Challenge every thought you have about yourself. Ask yourself "Is this really true? Am I really not good at this?"

Seek for the truth. Open yourself up to hear the Spirit and to tune into your own heart. Be self-aware, truly self-aware. I think at the end of this week, you will find the list is not as long as you once imagined it would be. If you aren't sure where to begin, start with a long brain dumping session and just write a big long list of all the things you think you aren't good at, no matter how big or how small. Just write it down. It's okay, this is just a starting place. Then go back through that list, one by one, and take each item to God.

First, ask yourself if you really aren't good at that thing, really get in touch with your own feelings, and then ask God what He thinks about it. Seek out the truth, not the lie you are tempted to tell yourself. As you go through the line items, if you find that you just can't feel at peace with thinking you aren't good at a certain item, admit to yourself that you actually *are* good at it, and scratch it off the list! Seriously, physically scratch it off your list with whatever writing utensil you have available. It can be very reinforcing to have that physical act of challenging a paradigm and acknowledging the truth.

Once you have gone through your list and scratched off all the things that just aren't true, what you should have left is a list of humble God-centered truths, and since you have involved Him in the process of questioning each and every item, you should actually feel some Divine peace at what is left on that list. Interesting feeling, isn't it? To feel peace in the things you aren't good at? That's the peace of humble truth. (If you don't feel at peace with the list you have left, go back through and see if there are still items on that list that you aren't resolved with. Most likely there are a few.)

We all have things we aren't good at, it's simply part of the human condition that God blessed us with. The key is to not make those things more than they are. Those things turn us toward each other, and most importantly, they turn us toward Him.

Congratulations, you are seeing yourself more truthfully, and you are loving yourself more celestially.

I'm not so good at...

Part Two,
Growth and Awakening

Second Chances

You are changing. You are not the same person you were when you began this journey. For the last 6 months you have spent weekly intentional time in open conversation with the one being who loves you more than any other. You have spent dedicated time with your celestial and eternal Father, drawing closer to Him through open and vulnerable conversation. You have shared deep hard pains, and light-hearted laughter, and you have torn down walls put into place by ages-old societal traditions and rules. You are learning to talk with Him with an open heart and an open mind, exactly how He wants you to.

For the second half of this journey, you will have the opportunity to repeat most of the topics you covered over the previous 6 months. You have grown and gained so much during that time. Now you will be able to address many of those topics with the new skills of vulnerability and honesty that you have developed over half a year of soul-searching work. You will be able to approach them as a more genuine and honest version of yourself.

In a way, you could look at Part One as a preparatory exercise to prepare you for Part Two, as warmups to opening night, so to speak. Just think about that very first week, that very first conversation, how would it be different now that you've been practicing open and vulnerable conversation for many months? I'm guessing it would be quite different now.

Don't misunderstand me, I don't want you to discount the work you have done over the last 6 months, every bit of it was real. Every conversation with God was real. Every awareness was real. And they were all necessary. The growth you have experienced in Part One is valid and integral to your journey towards true self-discovery and connection with your Creator. The conversations you had have helped to prepare you to have even deeper and more intimate conversations in the second part of this journey.

As you work through Part Two, take some time each week to look back in the book at the conversations you had the last time you had that week's topic. You may prefer to read your previous conversation before you write your new thoughts this time, or you may prefer to write your current thoughts uninfluenced by your previous conversation and then go back and review (this is what I recommend). Either way is fine. Just be sure to take some time and ponder the changes you are seeing in yourself and in your conversations with God this go around compared to the last. I think you will be pleased with your growth, I know God is.

As in Part One, be sure to approach each conversation with an open and honest heart. Truly let your feelings and thoughts flow. Truly let God into your deepest desires, worries, insights, and emotions. Tell Him everything without shame or reservation. After all, He already knows you, He just wants the opportunity to remind you that He loves you no matter what.

Ready? It's time for some real vulnerability.

You got this.

"Dear God…"

"Dear God, I always wanted to tell you…"

One more time, rip the bandaid off and get right to it. I want you to sit down and tell God something you have never told Him before. The topic of conversation can be either light or heavy, it really depends on what you're feeling this week, but if I were to encourage you one way or the other (if you really aren't feeling compelled in either direction), I would encourage you to go deep.

What is it that you've always wanted to tell Him that you never have?

What is it that's been sitting in the back of your mind, or in the deepest parts of your heart, that you've always wanted to bring out and put into words to Him? To the one who loves you most? To the one who is always there and doesn't care what you did or did not do?

When you say these words, "Dear God, I always wanted to tell you…" what feelings stir in your heart?

Is there something heavy that you've wanted to share with Him but just haven't? Something that you've held onto for years but just never felt the courage to speak out loud or to write down?

Or is it something lighter or something funny?

Take some time this week to really think about this, to really think about the things you've always wanted to tell Him but maybe felt like you couldn't, for whatever reason.

Often times societal constructs get in the way of our conversations with God. You may have been told that you *can't* say certain things to Him, or that you *shouldn't* say certain things to Him. This is your week to throw all that out the window. Challenge those messages this week and tell Him exactly what you've always wanted Him to know.

I always wanted to tell You...

"I'm mad at You because…"

This can be a really hard week for many people, because the very idea of being mad at God seems unrighteous or inappropriate. I understand that personally as I carried the same mentality for many years of my life. It wasn't until I really started to understand His perfect love for me that I started to understand that He was going to love me no matter what, even though there were things that I was very frustrated with Him over. There were angers that I was carrying in my heart, because of things in my life that had happened, or things that I didn't understand, and when I finally allowed myself to acknowledge that I was upset at God for a lot of those things, I found a whole new level of freedom with Him. The doors were swung wide open (or at least they were more open than they were before). This change gave me more freedom in truly talking to Him, and in return, I gained more freedom in truly *hearing* Him.

What I found through my anger was peace and understanding, because when I finally started to talk to Him about the things that I was mad at Him for, I really started to understand how His perfect love was taking affect in my life, and how those very things were placed in my life to help me grow and become a better, kinder, more loving person. It may sound counterintuitive to you, especially if you grew up in a society that shuns this level of open emotional sharing, but you *will* find peace through your anger. When you finally break free and allow yourself to share *all* emotions with Him, including your perceived "negative" emotions, you will find more peace than you ever knew was possible.

This week, I challenge you to truly be vulnerable in your conversations with God. Let Him have it, really. Tell Him how angry you are, and why. I promise you, He is there to hear you, I promise you that you will not get lost in your anger, rather you will find pieces of you that you had long forgotten.

He loves you, even when you're mad at Him.

I'm mad at You because...

"Why did You…?"

The big question: "Why did You?" This question has plagued humanity since the dawning of time. There are so many things we do not understand, so many pieces of God's greater puzzle that are just eluding our grasp. This week is the time to find closure, if possible. Take the time to really think about the events in your life that you don't understand, events that you still struggle to see God's hands in, and take those events to Him in prayer and in conversation. Ask Him why He did whatever it is He did. Ask Him why He allowed whatever it is He allowed. Or why He didn't do or didn't allow whatever it is He didn't do or didn't allow. His door is always open for you, ask Him whatever questions you need.

Heads up, as you sit and ponder this question this week, you will find that there are probably more times in your life that you want to ask Him about than you realize. So go for it. Open up the conversation with Him this week and ask Him why He did whatever it is you are wondering or concerned about. Get personal. Get it off your chest. Remove the burden from your shoulders. Let it all out.

You will find closure here, if you are open to what that closure may look like, because it may not come in the form that you had expected, or even hoped for. Sometimes closure comes from His reminder that His ways are higher than our ways and we just don't know everything He knows. Sometimes closure is found in simply trusting that He knows what He's doing.

He's got this, and He's got you.

Why did You...?

"Did You hear the one about…?"

Joke time! This week is a lighthearted and fun week. Sometimes we forget that we can talk to God in the good times as well as in the bad times, in the light times as well as in the dark times. This week is here to just remind you that He's always there and He always wants to hear from you, even when things are going great. We want to get to the point where we can share every emotion with Him, even laughter and excitement. You've worked pretty hard on tearing down barriers and learning to share deeper harder emotions with Him, so this week just have some fun and take some time to share your favorite jokes with Him (they don't all have to start with "Did you hear the one about…?"!). By the end of the week you should find yourself a little more comfortable to share a little more emotion with Him, even the silly emotions.

Did You hear the one about...?

"When I was a little child…"

We all have something in our past that brings us heartbreak and turmoil in our present. We all have something from our childhood that is confusing, hurtful, or even traumatic. This week is an opportunity for you to go back to your roots with God, to share with Him those things that you remember from the earliest years of your life that played a foundational role in who you are today and how your life is turning out. Some of those things are going to be good and happy memories, some of them will be the exact opposite.

I highly recommend you take some time before you sit down with Him to ponder on this statement: "When I was a little child…" If you've been writing your conversations down in the mornings, perhaps change to the evenings for this week and allow your mind a full day to ponder what things you want to talk to Him about from your childhood. Often we need that extra time for our minds to open themselves up to those old memories, because often we have *subconsciously* shut them down so that we don't *consciously* have to deal with them in our present adult lives, but just because we aren't consciously aware of them doesn't mean they aren't still affecting us.

Start each morning reminding yourself to think about things that happened when you were a little child; give yourself permission to go back there. Give yourself permission to open those memories back up again so that you can process them together with your Father in Heaven. Then let the process do its work. Trust that the memories will be there when you need them.

When the time comes that you have set apart to have this conversation, find a place where you can sit quietly, and then begin telling Him about whatever it is that comes to your mind. If you normally don't like to have your conversations with God out loud, that's fine, but maybe for this one at least vocalize the words, "When I was a little child," and then let your inner mind do the rest. You'll be surprised what happens when you just say those few words out loud. You'll be surprised at the memories that come.

Share them all with Him, He wants to hear them, because remember, He was there too.

When I was a little child...

"The last few years have been…"

The last few years have been… what? Have they been good? Have they been bad? Have they been awful? Have they been great?

How have things gone the last few years? You've spent some time talking about what life was like when you were little, so how's it going now? Did things happen in the last few years the way you expected them to? Or did they take an unexpected turn that you hadn't planned on? How exactly has life been going?

Most adults, when prompted with this sentence, will usually find that the last few years have been a little tough, but why is that? Why is life so often difficult as an adult? How would it have been different if you had a better, more open relationship with God throughout the last few years? Have those years really been as tough as you thought they were? Or could they have been better? All questions to ponder this week as you think about what you want to talk to God about the last few years.

Maybe the last few years have been really great, and you just want to tell Him thank you for that. Or maybe the last few years have really been tough and hard and you want to share your emotions about that with Him. Either way, just get real. Don't try to sugarcoat it, and don't try to over-inflate it. Be honest about what the last few years were really like, and talk to Him about it.

Then listen to hear His perspective.

These last few years have been...

"I always wished I had done…"

We hear a lot in the self development world that we shouldn't have regrets. Well, that's all fine and dandy, but it isn't realistic. Whether we should or shouldn't have them is irrelevant this week, because the truth of the matter is we usually do have them whether we admit it or not.

I fully agree with living life in the present and seeing our past experiences as steppingstones along our path to growth and peace; I believe that wholeheartedly and teach it often. However, that doesn't mean that the regrets we have just magically disappear. It's natural to have feelings of sadness and grief. Those are natural human emotions when we feel like we have missed out on something we wanted to take part in. The only way to resolve those emotions is to let ourselves feel them, to welcome them in, to love them while they're here, and then when the time comes, send them lovingly on their way.

No shaming yourself this week, okay? Share the things with God that you always wished you had done in your life. Share the events you wish you had attended, the topics you wish you had studied, the talents you wish you had developed, whatever it is that you wish you had always done, but never got a chance to. Open your heart to Him and share the memories, the thoughts, the feelings, and the regrets.

This doesn't have to be a deep and heavy week. Depending on where you are at, it may or may not be. If you aren't feeling deep heaviness about the things you wish you had always done, that's great. Go with that. Share with Him in a lighthearted manner.

Who knows? Maybe by sharing these things with Him this week, you will find the motivation and the opportunity to do some of them that are still available and turn them from regrets into accomplishments!

I always wished I had done...

"Something I don't understand is…"

I know I use this term a lot, but this week is a week of *vulnerability*. Many of us were brought up in cultures (religious cultures especially), that do not support the idea of questioning what you have been taught. Whether the religion itself preaches that mentality or not, it's often present in the culture that surrounds the religious teachings. If this applies to you, then this will be another week of challenging societal norms, of challenging the system.

Dedicate your conversations this week solely to the things you don't understand about His plan, and to the questions you have about the doctrine you've been taught. Only you can tell how strong the societal pull is within your heart and your mind, so only you will know how hard you're going to have to fight to ask those questions this week.

Perhaps it's easy for you to acknowledge the things that you don't understand in God's great plan; if so, I applaud you for that. This week will flow a little more easily for you. However, if you are like the many people who struggle with admitting that you don't understand all of the aspects of God's gospel, then this week may be a little bit harder for you in terms of opening up and really sharing your confusion with Him.

As in other weeks, I remind you that He loves you and that He wants to hear from you. There is no question you can ask Him that will offend Him. God does not have an ego. Anytime we come to Him is a time He cherishes. He knows we aren't perfect and He is ever patient with us.

You may find that you need a couple of days before you can actually sit down and have this conversation with Him, that's okay. When you get there, do the best you can to open the floodgates and let your feelings flow. Tell Him what it is you don't understand about His gospel and explain that you need some help coming to terms with some things. Again, be vulnerable and honest.

Also, remember that faith has a large component of "not knowing." It's okay if we don't understand everything, some things are just too big for us to understand. That doesn't mean that He doesn't want us to come to Him and ask Him about them. Give Him a chance this week. Give Him the chance to help you resolve some of your questions about His teachings (or the teachings you have been taught about Him by others).

Something I don't understand is...

"I'm struggling with…"

What is bothering you?

What is troubling your heart?

What are the things that are sitting in your subconscious that just can't seem to find resolution?

What are the roadblocks in your life right now?

Is there something you're struggling with mentally?

Emotionally?

Spiritually?

Are you struggling with something about yourself and your own identity?

Are you struggling to develop a certain skill or aptitude that you feel will make you successful?

Are you struggling with a portion of your faith?

Are there questions that you have about God and His gospel that you just can't seem to reconcile?

Do you worry that you are weak, or that you in someway don't match up to the perceived standards of the world?

(Or the perceived standards of what it *looks like* to live a God-centered life?)

Be open and honest with God this week about whatever it is you are struggling with. Remember not to shame yourself or your worries, no concern is too small for Him. He loves all parts of you. Give Him a chance to hear you, and then give Him a chance to send you peace.

I'm struggling with...

"I'm looking forward to…"

This week is a bit of a change of pace from the previous weeks. You've had a lot of really deep discussions with God lately and I'm sure many of those have been pretty heavy. That's good, those are often the conversations that we really need to have in order to tear down the walls inside of us that keep us from truly being vulnerable with Him and coming to understand our own worth. That being said, we want to change things up a little bit this week.

Our relationship with God is not meant to only be heavy; in fact, it's meant to be joyful. The heavy discussions are some of the keys that open the doors to a more joyful God-centered existence by allowing us to finally be fully vulnerable, but those are not the only conversations we need to be having. This week is about hope.

Like other weeks, this may be easy for you, or it may be hard for you, depending on where you are right now on your spiritual journey. If you are in a hopeful, forward-looking place, great, share everything with Him that you are excited for regarding the future. If however, you are struggling with the present, then the future is likely to look bleak and feel even bleaker, and this may be a harder topic for you to tackle. That's okay. Remember never to shame yourself for the way you are currently feeling. Just get curious about it instead.

If you're struggling with the future, take some time before writing your conversations with God this week to meditate, ponder, and even daydream about a hopeful future. The future isn't set in stone, and often all it takes for the hope and happiness wheels to be set in motion is for us to bring our desired goodness into the light. Meditating, pondering, and dreaming are all tools we have at our disposal to bring our deep hopes from the darkness of our hidden minds into the light of possibility and potential.

Start each day with this sentence in mind: "God, I'm really looking forward to…," and you may be surprised at what will emerge from places in your heart that you didn't know were there.

I'm looking forward to...

"These next few years are going to be…"

Another forward looking week. However, this week is without any sort of emotional prompting. I'm not going to prompt you with "looking forward…" or "struggling with…," or anything that will lead you one way or another. This week is a blank canvas where your spirit can paint whatever picture it feels. This is an opportunity for you to get in tune with yourself without much prompting from me.

When you say the words out loud "These next few years are going to be…" what emotions arise within you? Where in your body are you feeling those emotions? Pay attention to you body. Our bodies manifest emotions physically; that's literally why we call them "feelings." Practicing physical awareness can help you sift through the noise of the world and really tune in to what it is you are actually feeling. With that in mind, what sensations arise in the physical part of your being when you ponder this week's conversation?

Helpful questions to ponder:
Do you feel excited about the next couple of years?
Do you feel worried about the next few years?
Where do you notice these feelings in your body?
What do they feel like?
Do you feel a tingling or warming sensation somewhere?
Do you feel tension anywhere?
Do you feel a rushing sensation or an increased heart rate?
Do you feel nauseated?
Are you smiling?
Are you tired and worn out?

Or are you restless and filled with energy?

Most of the time we mortals are very out of touch with how our emotions manifest themselves physically. We often have too much going on around us, too much stimulation, to allow us to really focus inwardly and on our own experiences. Opening your spiritual eyes to the sensations that arise in your body with certain emotions can really help you tune in on exactly what it is you are feeling.

I know what it's like to be confused about my feelings. When I learned to be more aware of the physical sensations that partnered with the emotions I was feeling, it really helped me to sift through the messiness of life around me and become more aware of what it is I was actually feeling in those moments. This week let your body talk to your spirit about the feelings you carry deep down inside of you about the future. Then tell God what you came up with.

Again, blank canvas here. What do the next few years look like and feel like to you? Tell God all about it.

He already knows what the next few years are going to bring of course, but He wants to know what you think about it, and how you feel about it.

These next few years are going to be...

"I felt alone when…"

Loneliness is one of the heaviest feelings we can experience in this mortal life. Loneliness is often a strange phenomenon for us humans because we always seem to be physically surrounded by other people, and yet even in the midst of the crowds and the hustle and bustle of life, we often feel very very alone. Loneliness is a universal feeling, which is somewhat ironic if you think about it. Everyone knows what it feels like to feel alone, and you would think that would help us all to have something to come together over, but yet loneliness still prevails.

When have you felt lonely?

Do you feel lonely now?

Why?

What's going on inside of you?

When you felt alone, what other feelings were you carrying at the same time?

What was the situation?

Were you surrounded by people and yet still felt as if you were metaphorically "alone on a deserted island?"

What was that like for you?

Were you able to come out of it?

If so, how?

Is there anything you learned during that time about yourself?

Any personal awarenesses?

Tell God about it. Tell Him everything. He knows what it feels like to feel alone. After all, He is the one that gave us the capacity to feel all of these emotions. There is no one better to hear you and comfort you in your loneliness than Him.

Bonus question: Have you ever pondered why God would allow us to feel lonely? Why we all have to feel alone at some point in our lives? It's an interesting question; one that most people have never truly pondered, at least not with the intent to learn. If you haven't ever done so, this week would be a good week to ask God what He thinks about it.

I felt alone when...

"I knew You were with me when…"

This week is the opposite side of the coin from loneliness, and serves as a natural outgrowth of your conversation last week. Who knows? In your conversation last week, you may have even found ways that He was with you in the midst of your loneliest times. If so, I applaud you, that's a beautiful thing. If not, that's okay. You had the conversation with Him last week that you needed to have, and that's exactly what it needed to be. You will have many more opportunities to talk with Him and to learn to see Him in your life, even in the darkest times. This week, focus on the opposite of loneliness, focus on presence.

When have you felt Him in your life?

When have you felt His presence?

When did you know that He was with you?

If you want to take that even further, how did you know that He was with you?

He has promised to always be with us, but it's not always easy to feel the manifestation of that promise (hence the "lonely" conversation last week), but this week is a chance for you to share with Him the times when you knew He was walking side-by-side with you down the path. Those are important memories and He would love to share in reminiscing about those times with you. Similar to a few weeks ago, this is a blank canvas.

What were the times like when you knew He was with you?

Were they good times?

Bad times?

Both?

Often we notice His presence best in the trying times because those are the times we are looking for Him most. If those are the times that you remember Him being with you, talk to Him about those times. Tell Him what you remember and how you knew He was with you.

For a challenge, try thinking about both difficult *and* easy times. Even though we tend to notice Him most in the difficult times, He is also with us in the easy times. We just tend to forget Him when life is going great. Try to find some times in your memory when you knew He was with you even when life was full of happiness and peace.

It's good for us to recognize His presence at all times, and not just when we feel like we need Him most.

I knew You were with me when...

"I'm worried about…"

Worry is a complex emotion, especially in religious cultures, because we are often subliminally taught that worry is bad because in some way worry shows a lack of faith. In some cultures the shame isn't even subliminal, it's right out in the open. That situation can be very conflicting for us, because just because people say "don't worry," doesn't mean worry magically goes away. Worrying is part of our default human experience. The problem is most people try to "encourage" those around them to not worry by trying to shame the worry out of them. This simply doesn't work.

We all worry. I do, every day. I'm getting better at it, but it's still there. The ironic thing with these types of topics is that the most effective way to stop worrying, begins with actually accepting and admitting that we are indeed worrying. When we accept ourselves just the way we are, it opens doors for us to elevate to entirely new levels.

This week I want you to start with openly accepting and allowing yourself to worry. Then take the most important step: Take those worries to God. Let Him know what it is you are carrying, what it is you are worried about. Just ramble it all out to Him, I promise He will never shame you for it. He already knows you're worried, so there's no sense in hiding it.

What are you worried about?

Is it something to do with your family?

Your friends?

Yourself?

Is it something to do with the world around you?

Politics?

Pop-culture?

School, work, or home duties?

Tell Him everything, let Him be in that worry with you, let Him walk that path with you, let Him guide you and comfort you. True peace comes from Him, but we will never know and be grateful for that peace unless we accept and share our worries and fears. Challenge the voices in your head, challenge the societal pressure, and just let yourself be.

Whatever it is, this week is a chance for you to just let it all flow with the one who loves you most.

I'm worried about...

"I'm so grateful for…"

Another opportunity for a "heart dump" this week. Last week you had the opportunity to tell God what was weighing on your heart, this week is the flip side of that discussion. What are the things in your life that you are grateful for that maybe you never expressed to Him?

Take a deep breath and close your eyes for just a moment. Try to clear your mind from all the hustle and bustle of the day. Now open your eyes and take a look around you. See how blessed you are. If you allow yourself, you will see an abundance of blessings right before your eyes. Blessings you experience every single day.

Do you have clothes?

Do you have electricity?

Do you have water?

What do you see in just the room you are currently sitting in?

How are those things blessings to you?

Now take the next moment to express gratitude to God for the all the blessings you see and feel. It doesn't matter how simple you may feel the blessing is, share your gratitude for it with Him. Even if all you can say is, "Thank you," that's enough.

Note: It's okay to ask Him for inspiration on how to share your blessings with those who aren't as fortunate as you are, but that's not the purpose of this week. It's often difficult for us to just be grateful for what we have without shaming ourselves because we have more than someone else. That happens a lot in religious cultures. It's a good thing to want to bless others and to want others to have blessed easy peaceful lives, but this week is about you putting aside shame and expressing gratitude for what you have.

There will come a time and a place to ask for inspiration on how to help others, but this week I want you to just focus on *your* life and the blessings that surround *you* each and every day. Think about your body, your mind, your spirit, your lifestyle, your friends, your family, your job, your education, your hobbies and activities, and anything else you can think of where you can see blessings.

It's okay if you don't feel gratitude in all of those areas right now, they're just suggestions to help you start to think about the different ways that God has blessed you in this life. This week, take time to just say, "Thank you." Tell Him what you're grateful for. It doesn't matter if it's some huge life-changing thing or if it's as simple as seeing your favorite ice cream flavor at the grocery store. (What an amazing blessing that is!)

Open your heart and let the gratitude flow. You'll be amazed at how good you feel at the end of this week.

I'm so grateful for...

"I can't seem to find peace because…"

We live in very turbulent times. It seems that every day news reports and social media posts highlight another disagreement, another argument, and/or another fight between various groups of people who subscribe to different ways of thinking. These reports and posts send a message that our world is constantly divided and ever in turmoil. So many of us struggle to find peace in our lives because of this never ending onslaught of negativity and division in the world around us.

However, maybe the lack of peace you are currently feeling stems from something a bit closer to home for you than the national and world news. Perhaps there is discord in your own family. Or perhaps there is discord within your own soul.

What is it that is making you restless?

What is it that has stolen your hope for peace?

Is it the noise in the world around you?

Or is it something more intimate and private?

God has promised us peace when we turn to Him, but for most of us that can be a pretty elusive promise. His peace is different than our peace. His peace is grounded in an eternal perspective, a perspective that knows all things and how all things will progress. You and I do not have that same eternal perspective, simply because we are mortal.

Talk to Him this week about the restlessness you are feeling. Really dig into the reasons that you just can't seem to find peace in your life.

What is it that keeps you up at night?

What is it that worries you in the back of your mind all day long?

Be open and vulnerable with Him this week about your difficulties finding calm and rest so you can begin to find the path to the peace you seek.

I can't seem to find peace because...

"I felt so peaceful when…"

In contrast to the restlessness you talked to God about last week, this week take some time to ponder on the times in your life when you *did* feel peace.

What was happening?

What was the world like around you?

Was it any different?

Or were *you* different?

If so, why?

What was different about you in the times when you felt at peace?

Was there something happening inside of you then that isn't now?

Did you have a different relationship with God then than you do now?

We know that the world cannot bring us peace, it will forever be in turmoil due to its ever-changing and imperfect nature. Peace comes from within. Peace comes from our ability to communicate with God, and to hear His voice. Peace comes from being in His presence where we know that everything will work out exactly as it is meant to be. In His presence we are reminded that because He loves us eternally, everything in our lives is meant to one day bring us true and everlasting joy.

As you ponder this week about the times when you felt peaceful, ponder about *why* you felt peaceful in those times vs. the times where you felt restless. Focus on what was going on inside you rather than what was happening around you. As you talk to God about the times when you felt peaceful, ask Him to help you understand why you felt that way, and how you can maintain that feeling in your life.

Remembering and understanding the peaceful times will help you better find peace in the restless tumultuous times.

I felt so peaceful when...

"What do You want me to do about…?"

Him? Her? It? That situation that happened last week? That situation that's coming up soon? That work situation? That home situation?

What are you unsure about and need help/guidance with? It doesn't have to be anything big; remember, God wants to hear from us in all things. He cares about every detail of our lives, no matter how big or how small.

If there is something in your life that you don't know how to handle at the moment, talk to Him about it. Ask Him what He wants you to do about it. Then listen for His answer.

There are three steps in this conversation that are all equally important: talking, listening, and doing. If you struggle with the talking part, with asking for help and advice, then this is an opportunity for you to practice opening up and expressing your confusion or worry about life in a safe place. There is no safer place than God. This week, practice asking Him for advice. You will learn to hear and see His answers in time.

If on the other hand, you are pretty good at asking others for help, then focus this week on the *listening* and *doing* steps. Ask Him what He wants you to do, then be quiet and listen for His answers. If nothing comes right away, keep your eyes open and look for His answers in your life around you. Often He sends answers through other people, so make sure you are paying attention when interacting with others.

Once you receive an answer, get up and do it! If you ask Him what He wants you to do about something, and He tells you, then it's on you to make it happen. Hop to it, and do it. (Reminder: if you are scared to do what He asks, it's totally okay to ask Him for courage. He won't leave you alone.)

Again, this doesn't have to be something huge this. In fact, if you aren't used to asking for help, it's probably best to start with something small until you feel more comfortable. Either way, no matter how big or how small the issue, He wants to help so be sure to look and listen for His answers. Once you start to recognize His answers, you will start to see them more and more in your everyday life.

Eventually, you will see Him everywhere.

What do You want me to do about...?

"Why did _____ have to happen?"

We all have events in our lives, that we just don't know what to do with. Sometimes things happen that seem so far outside our understanding of God's plan that they can prove very shaking to our faith. Sometimes, because those events can be so confusing and painful, they end up being the very reason that we don't talk to Him anymore.

Some things are just too difficult for us to understand in the moment and that's what this week is all about. It's about the big confusions. It's about those events that happened in your life or in the lives of those around you that you just can't come to terms with, that you just can't seem to reconcile with your understanding of God and His nature.

First of all, give yourself permission to be confused. It's okay. Sometimes, living and growing up in very religious cultures can have a stifling effect on our vulnerability with God because we adopt the false belief that we are never allowed to have questions. I am telling you right now, *it's okay to not know the reasons for everything*, it doesn't mean that you are any less faithful. It doesn't mean that you are sinning or bad in someway. It simply means that you are human, and because you are human, it's sometimes difficult to see with an eternal perspective and understand how everything fits into a grand eternal plan.

Be patient and compassionate with yourself, especially in the areas where you feel most tender, which often include the types of situations where you just don't know why something had to happen. Be ready for some tears this week. This may be a hard week for you as you acknowledge those feelings and hard memories that are still lurking in the back of your mind. It's time to shed light on them and ask God to give you some peace and some understanding about why those events had to happened.

Just remember, I know this is hard, but remember that you may not get the answers you seek. Remember that His ways are not our ways, and sometimes the things that He needs to do are just too big for us to fully understand. That is why we are asked to have faith. Sometimes we just need to believe that everything happens for a reason, and leave it at that. If that's the case for you this week, if you don't get an answer to your question about why something had to happen the way it happened, then ask Him for peace instead.

Cry those tears out with Him. Ask Him all the questions. And then in the end, ask Him for help to believe that all things happen for our good, even the things you don't understand.

Then ask Him for help to let it go.

You got this.

Why did _____ have to happen?

"I love it when You…"

Finally, a happy week, right? After last week, you may need it to regain some sanity! Share some happiness with God this week. Let Him know what you think and feel about the good times in your life.

What are you grateful to Him for doing for you?

What does He do in your life that puts a smile on your face every time it happens?

Share those moments with Him this week. Fair warning, you may struggle with this for a bit, and that's okay. It's human nature to not consciously dwell on the good things in our lives. We are more wired to see and remember the location of a poisonous spider in our garden than to remember the locations of all the beautiful flowers. Don't shame yourself if you need a few minutes to come up with the good times.

Remembering and sharing positivity is a muscle that all of humanity needs to exercise; it just doesn't come easy to most of us. The good thing is once the good memories start flowing, they will begin to flow more and more easily, which will have a lasting positive effect on your life. If you need to, start with something small: "I love it when You wake me up two minutes before the alarm clock so I don't get startled awake." "I love it when You send spring rainstorms to water the flowers." "I love it when You nudge me to say hi to someone on the street so they can know they aren't alone."

Ponder this week on the things you love that God does for you, and then be ready to have the happiness floodgates thrown open! Happiness begets happiness. Gratitude begets gratitude. The more things you come up with to tell Him you love, the more your brain will start to rewire towards a more positive mindset. And, since you are involving Him in this process, you are essentially invoking His power which will make those brain changes even more effective and long-lasting. I love that benefit of consecrating everything we do (and think), to Him. When we turn to Him, He gives us His power to make everything just work better. Pretty cool, huh?

So, what do you love that He does for you? Tell Him everything you come up with.

This will be a beautiful week for you.

I love it when You...

"Please help me understand…"

A few weeks ago you spent some time talking to God about why certain things had to happen in your life, or in the lives of others. You discussed things and events that you struggled to understand the meaning behind. A few weeks before that you asked him about doctrinal teachings you struggle to understand. In both of those conversations you practiced being open with Him about your questions and your insecurities, and you practiced understanding that having questions does not mean you lack faith, in fact asking questions is often how we build faith: exercised faith, not blind ignorant faith.

God does not want us to be ignorant. He does not want us to blindly follow Him, never learning His ways or getting to know His nature. Of course He wants us to trust Him if something comes up that is too big for us to understand, but He wants that trust to be exercised, to be used, not to be left ignorant and passive.

God wants us to build strong faith that will resist the test of time because we put the effort into building it. Blind faith is weak faith, and eventually will fail. He wants us to ask the questions so He can answer the ones we can understand, and so He can reassure us on the ones we can't.

This is another week of questioning. The previous topics were specifically about past events and doctrinal teachings that you don't understand, this week is much broader. This week is about *anything* you don't understand.

Is there something to do with the world around you that He created that you don't understand?

Something about the future and His plan of salvation and exaltation?

Is there something going on with a loved one in your life that you don't understand?

Something with work?

Or home?

Is it all of these things?

Whatever it is, take it to Him this week. Continue with the energy of open vulnerability that you have been building for weeks now.

Remember, it's not a sin to not understand.

Please help me understand...

"I don't know what to feel about…"

Numb…

We all know what it feels like to not feel anything. We know what it feels like to feel numb, to not know how we feel about a certain event, topic, discussion, principle, etc. We all know what it feels like to feel confused about our feelings. (That's a lot of feeling in our "not feeling" huh?)

It's okay. It's part of the process. Awakening is hard. Self-awareness is hard. Challenging societal norms is hard.

Before you started to open your spiritual eyes there were probably many things you felt simply because someone else told you to feel them. Our society loves to tell us what to think and how to feel, and frankly, many of us love to be told; it's easier that way. But it isn't happier.

Our spirits will never find peace in such a primal, basic state. We are meant to elevate. We are meant to grow, to learn, to feel. This week may involve some paradigm challenging for you. Get in tune with your spirit, with your soul, and seek out those places where you aren't really at peace with what you are being told to feel, the places where the "popular crowd" is telling you to feel a certain way but you just can't get on board.

Take those feelings and situations to God and ask *His* opinion on them. Ask for help to understand your real feelings, the feelings underneath all the noise from the world. Accept whatever comes. Remember, feelings are neither good nor bad, they just are. Don't judge your feelings, don't try to change them, just look for them and accept them. Take the situation to God, and ask for help to understand how you really feel.

Important Note: If the feelings that arose in you when you first read this week's prompt came from more of a traumatized place rather than a confused place, pay attention to that. Numbness can come for many reasons, and if you aren't feeling confused about societal paradigms, childhood messages, or the like, rather you are feeling numb because of a certain traumatic event that your mind and soul just can't come to terms with, take that awareness as a message that God wants you to heal from that trauma. It's okay to explore that with Him. However, you may want to also explore that with a trained professional. Therapy is a gift from God in many ways, I know mine has been.

Be kind to yourself. If you feel you need it, find someone trained to listen to your hurt, someone who will help walk you down the path of healing and peace. You deserve it.

I don't know what to feel about...

"Thank You for teaching me about…"

What is something that you are glad you know about now, that you didn't know about 10 years ago? 15 years ago?

Or even something you didn't know about yesterday, last week, or last month?

What is some bit of knowledge that has changed your life?

That has changed the way you see yourself, your fellow spiritual brothers and sisters, or the world the itself?

How has gaining this knowledge changed you?

What has happened differently in your life now that your eyes are opened?

Ponder this week on the things God has taught you about that have really had an impact on your life and your spirituality. Focus on knowledge, wisdom, awarenesses, etc. Don't focus on abilities or on things you are grateful for learning how to *do*, that's for next week. This week is for understandings, for wisdom gained, for knowledge that has changed your life.

If something immediately comes to mind, great, tell Him all about it and how grateful you are for it. If you're drawing a blank at the moment, that's okay. It often takes time to rewire our brains to focus more on the positives in our lives, so be kind to yourself it nothing comes quickly.

Grab out a piece of paper and a pen and start writing down awarenesses you have had throughout your life about yourself and about life in general. You will be surprised how things will start to flow once you put that pen to paper. So start writing and let them flow.

You'll know when something comes up that you want to talk to Him about, just pay attention to your feelings as you are writing. Once you have something, tell Him all about it. Tell Him why you are grateful for His teaching and how your life is better because of what you now know.

As with all the other weeks, this week is a week of self-awareness, but it's also a week of gratitude. Focus on just telling Him thank you this week. Try to stave off any questioning, complaining, or pleading. There is a time and a place for those things, but this week is for gratitude.

Sharing gratitude with God is a very enlightening experience, so open your heart with gratitude, and let the light in.

Thank You for teaching me about...

"Thank You for teaching me how to…"

As I mentioned last week, this week is about things God has taught you how to do, rather than things He has taught you to know or understand. This week is about sharing your gratitude for things you have learned how to do that have had a substantial impact on your life. As with other weeks, be careful not to get lost in "the big things," or the skills the world finds value in. Those things are great, and if you have some of them, fantastic; definitely include them in your gratitude conversations with God this week. But more often than not, those aren't the skills that benefit your life the most.

Most often the skills God has taught us that allow us to function in the quiet times are the ones that benefit our lives the most:

The skill to truly listen to someone and hear that person's story.

The skill of tuning into your own feelings and knowing your own heart.

The ability to know your personal worth in a sea of confusing values set by the world.

The skill to laugh instead of cry.

The skill to cry instead of laugh.

The skill of sitting quietly and feeling wonder in the world around you.

The skill to see good in others, especially when they are struggling to see it in themselves.

The skill of seeing light and purpose, when all around you seems dark.

All these amazing skills that God has taught you, often through very difficult times of your own. Whatever it is, share some gratitude with God for teaching you how to do it. Big or small. Light or heavy. Outward or inward. It doesn't matter what it is, if you are grateful you learned how to do it, then share that gratitude with Him.

This is going to be a wonderful conversation for you this week, I can feel it.

Thank You for teaching me how to...

Part Three,
Love and Gratitude

The Last Part, or The First

You have reached the final part of this year-long journey, which isn't a final part at all really, rather it is just the beginning of the next part of your path to peace and happiness. One more step in your eternal journey of growth and discovery, in your eternal journey of love and light. These next two weeks are going to be different than the conversations you have had over the last eleven and a half months. You will find them to be simultaneously simple, and incredibly profound. These two conversations are the perfect culmination of the work and effort you have put into becoming an entirely new being, a being who is connected to God and yourself in ways that weren't possible a year ago.

Ready? Breath deeply, and enjoy.
You got this.
"Dear God…"

"I Love You."

That's it. "I love you." One week of just telling Him that you love Him. One week of simply sharing the love you have in your heart for your Father who loves you infinitely. The conversations you have been having with God have most likely become a part of your regular life now, so there is no need for a prompt to get your mind going anymore. While you're talking to Him each day, make a specific point of telling Him you love Him.

As often as the thought pops into your mind, or the feeling arises in your heart, simply say, "Hey God? I love you."

I love You...

"Thank You for loving me."

The final week. The final conversation. Perhaps the simplest and yet the most profound. Gratitude and love. Gratitude *for* love. Love is what it is all about. Love is what this journey is all about. You have now opened up to Him about every deep part of your soul you can find, and you have learned to feel His love for you through it all, dark times and light times alike.

This week all you need to do is thank Him for that love. Each day, thank Him for loving you. And while you're at it, be sure to thank yourself a time or two this week for loving you as well, because that is the secret surprise at the end of this journey. You haven't only built a better and stronger relationship with your Father in Heaven, you have simultaneously built a better and stronger relationship with yourself. Pretty cool, huh? That's worth being happy about.

Gratitude is the perfect way to end this chapter in your great story. Gratitude and love.

I can't even tell you how excited I am for you.

"Dear God, thank you for loving me."

("And dear me, thank you for loving me too!")

Thank You for loving me...

Final Thoughts

Ponder

Two questions:
Who were you a year ago?
Who are you now?

Even through all the crazy twists and turns of the past year, through all the emotional ups and downs, through all the spiritual highs and lows, through every step you have taken on this journey, the answer is simple: You are a different person now. You have grown in depth, in light, in knowledge, in experience, and most importantly, in love. You are a *new* person now. You have been renewed and remade through the increased levels of love you have gained from the real, honest, and vulnerable conversations you have had with God, and through the new levels of awareness and love He has helped you find for yourself.

A year has passed on this journey, an entire year. Think of that for just a moment. Think of the adventure you have had over the past 52 weeks as you have learned to open your heart and mind and share the deepest parts of yourself with the one who made you just the way He wants you to be. Think of the conversations you have had, of the depths you have traversed. Think of the heights and awarenesses you have come to. Think of the new levels of vulnerability and honesty that have become a part of this new version of you now.

Think of the love you have felt throughout this journey. Think of the love you have felt for God, for yourself, and for those around you who helped shape you into the new being you are today. Think of the love you are feeling right now. And most importantly, as the culmination of this entire process, think about where that love comes from, and what all of this really means:

"God is love. Whoever lives in love lives in God, and God in them." (1 John 4:16 NIV)

Thank you for joining me, what a ride it has been.

On to your next journey.

Ready?

You got this.

Love,
Blake

Also Available from Blake Wm. Halladay

ascend

30 Days to Respecting and Loving Yourself!

The YOUniversity Press

About The Author

Blake Wm. Halladay is an eclectic curator of all things happy, good, and loving. Blake has dedicated his life to helping others understand their true worth and find lasting happiness by discovering their innate ability for spirituality and growth. He lives near the shores of the Great Salt Lake with his family, a fluffy-faced pup, a few furry critters, and lots of goofball fish.

Follow Blake's journey at :
blakewmhalladay.com

Instagram and Facebook:
@blakewmhalladay

Made in United States
Orlando, FL
29 December 2023